The Dark Tunnel of Grief

Anna Veal

AuthorHouse™
1663 Liberty Drive
Bloomington, IN 47403
www.authorhouse.com
Phone: 1-800-839-8640

© 2009 Anna Veal. All rights reserved.

No part of this book may be reproduced, stored in a retrieval system, or transmitted by any means without the written permission of the author.

First published by AuthorHouse 8/24/2009

ISBN: 978-1-4490-1679-1 (e)
ISBN: 978-1-4490-1681-4 (sc)
ISBN: 978-1-4490-1680-7 (hc)

Printed in the United States of America
Bloomington, Indiana

This book is printed on acid-free paper.

Introduction

This book is written to share with you a life experience that caused me to walk through the grief process relying on one of Christ's most powerful tools – prayer. It took much time, rewriting, and prayer before I found the confidence needed to actually share my story. I remember the day I first felt led to write my story. My family and I recently moved to a new area and began attending a local church. While at a ladies event there – Knowing only a few ladies involved in the production - I decided to make a new acquaintance. I saw a lady sitting by herself and asked if I could join her. We had a twenty-minute conversation that felt like a three-hour intimate discussion. You know, God puts people in our lives for a reason. This lady shared with me her recent loss of a marriage and I spoke briefly about my loss of marriage and the death of my daughter. "We need to trust in the Lord through these tough times," I told her reassuringly. At the end of our conversation she replied, "You really helped me; thank you, I enjoyed our conversation." We sat together that day and enjoyed our brief, but special time with one another. Although God did not allow our paths to cross again, this providential relationship sparked my soul to share the victory I received after experiencing a long, dark journey.

Her words of thanks echoed loudly through my head; I could not quiet them. Maybe, I should share my experience with others, I thought. After all, it was the support and encouragement of others that helped me through my loss. I could no longer deny the call to write about my journey through grief and tell how prayer played such an instrumental part on my path to victory. I believe, God wants me to carry on this comfort by sharing my story with you. Remember dear brothers and sisters, Christ is awesome and does have a unique plan for each of us.

The Lord provided many tools for us to live a successful Christian life today. I found two powerful tools that worked for me: prayer and prayer journaling. Prayer allowed me to spend time with God and utter my deepest feelings to him. It was exactly what I needed during this tough, tragic time. Prayer journaling was simply a way to write out my prayers in a journal. By writing them out, it kept me focused on what I need to say. I have provided journal space at the end of each chapter so that you can journal your own prayers, thoughts and feelings as we journey together through the grief process.

Although I walk in victory today, my journey was like living in a long dark tunnel with no light at the end. As I experienced many stages of grief and started to work through the process, I found there truly was light at the end of the tunnel. You too can experience that light and how to reach it for yourself! Come along with me as you travel through your own grief journey. My prayer is that you will find the light at the end just as I finally did.

Table of Contents

Introduction	v
Dawn is Missing	1
Knock at The Door	6
The Phone Calls	12
Planning the Funeral	19
Lonely Days Ahead	28
Facing Reality with God's Blessings	33
Grief a Daily Struggle	42
Trying to Survive	51
The First Year	57
Special People in our Lives	65
Milestones	71
Dealing With Anger	79
Where Is My Brain?	87
Health and Fitness	95
Are Christians Pain Free?	101
Acknowledgements	113
This Book is Dedicated In Loving Memory of:	114

Dawn is Missing

My story began on a cool, crisp, clear, autumn night in Colorado. If you had ever been in Colorado, you know what I mean by cool, crisp, and clear. The time was around 9:00 pm and I was cleaning and preparing our home for the birthday celebrations that would take place that weekend.

My daughter had attended about seven weeks of college and was coming home to celebrate for the weekend. Prior to her leaving UNC Greeley, Colorado, she called me. "Mom," she said, "Don't wait up for me and don't try to call. My phone is dead and is on the car charger. I am stopping by to see Curtis (her boyfriend of almost four years) and then I will spend tonight with Dad, I will see you tomorrow for the party." I replied, "Okay, I love you!" "I love you too, Mom," she said.

Dawn was always good about telling me her plans and who she would be with, so I would not worry. Those of you who are parents know what I mean.

My son (Dawn's younger brother Adam) said, "Mom, Dad just called and said that Dawn has not arrived yet!" This caused me to have this huge panic attack. She should have arrived at his home no later than 7:30 or so. I called her boyfriend to see if he had heard from her. Curtis did not hear from her and had a sick feeling about the situation. I immediately made calls to the many highway patrols from Greeley, Colorado to Colorado Springs, and to area hospitals. As I was dialing, I thought, Dawn is going to bounce through the door and have a fit that I went to that extreme to call the highway patrol and hospitals. The highway patrol said there have been several accidents tonight but none involving your daughter's car. I was almost gasping for air. The hospitals had no record of her being brought in. Where else would I turn? I called her boyfriend back and his voice was at a tone I had never heard before. He said, "I do not have a good feeling about this!" I was silent and did not know what to say or do. I remembered her saying that she was taking a friend home in Black Forrest, Colorado, but I did not know her friend's phone number. Just as I thought I would pass out in fear, I heard a knock at the door.

Dawn & Adam June 2001

Dawn & Curtis

The Dark Tunnel of Grief

Journal
Date: _____

Anna Veal

Knock at The Door

I was sitting on the steps, inside our home, just a few feet away from the door when I heard a knock. I jumped up swung open the door, and yelled, "Where is she?" "It's my daughter, Dawn Marie. Take me to her. Take me now!" The look on their faces, I will not forget. The look was blank; their eyes were like three lost puppy dogs just begging me for mercy. The women in the middle spoke first. She said, "We can't. I'm sorry. May we come in?" I yelled back, "Take me to her now! I can handle it; take me!" Again she replied, "We can't; may we come in?" I proceeded to let them in. The women in the middle who was the coroner said, "There has been a terrible accident involving your daughter and her friend. Please mam, please sit." She noticed I was pregnant and she did not want me to pass out or fall. The coroner continued to tell us as much as she could about the accident. I wanted proof that this was really my daughter. Without showing me her body, how could she prove it? She handed me a picture and made sure she prepared me for what I would see. The picture was my baby! Her face was a little swollen and her front tooth chipped but it was *my* Dawn Marie. The coroner explained that the girls had been killed instantly and no opportunity was possible to transport them to a hospital. They were both pronounced dead at the scene. "They did not feel pain as they were killed on impact," she said. I still do not understand how someone can tell you that no pain was felt when they were not the ones involved. I know that our bodies shut down prior to impact; I guess that is what they were trying to tell me.

Oh my God, why have you forsaken me? I thought we had a deal! Why my little girl? Why, Lord? I asked you to protect her! I asked you to let her have a long life of happiness and joy! Why Lord, why? Dawn Marie was awesome! She had love, determination, motivation, passion and the list can go on and on. Why Lord? My head is spinning right now! I want to run away and go far, far away! How can I go on living for one more minute without my little girl, Lord? How, Lord?

Being pregnant, people always like to ask, "Is this your first? How many children do you have?" How will I begin to answer this? Will I answer, "I have one son

13, one daughter **DEAD,** and this one on the way!" Just what will I say?

Father God, what do I say? How will I answer this? What is the answer you want me to say? Help me, Lord Jesus, help me!

The Lord did not answer me that night. I would not have heard him anyway if he did because I was not listening. Although the Lord's presence felt as though his arms were wrapped tightly around me, holding me, and rocking me and telling me, everything was going to be ok, the emptiness I felt inside was laying heavy on my heart. I do not see how anything could ever be ok again! My life will never be the same again! I will never be able to smile again! My joy is gone forever!

My son Adam, who was only 13, had a huge burden to carry that night. I was so messed up and frozen that he had to call his dad and tell him what happen. I believe Adam did not have to say much; his dad knew it was not good news. The minute Adam called his dad; he came over right away to be with us and to help make phone calls.

Anna Veal

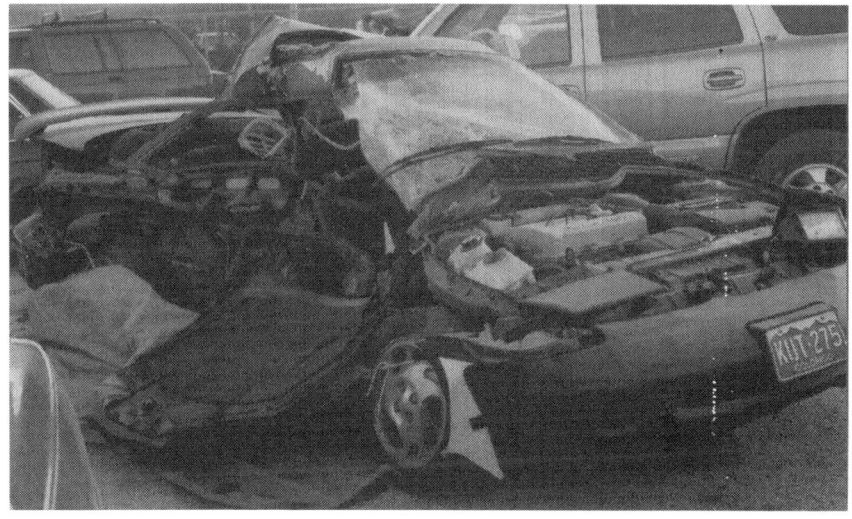

The Dark Tunnel of Grief

Journal

Date: _____

Anna Veal

The Phone Calls

We all made phone calls that night. The cell phones and house phone were all in use letting family and close friends know what had happened. My nephew called weeping and said with a shaky voice, "This should have been me, not Dawn!" "Dawn was a good girl; I am the one who drives stupidly!" We talked, and I cannot tell you what was said, but it was not my nephew's time, thank God! God has a time and day for each of us. **Ecclesiastes 3:2 states, "A time to be born and a time to die, a time to plant and a time to uproot."** This was not my nephew's time, but Dawn Marie's. I trust my nephew took a long look at his life that night and made some different choices when driving a vehicle. This accident was not caused by Dawn, but by the road, which was torn up and had no warning signs posted. Local residence had been calling the county requesting signs to be posted and repairs to be made on the road. If not, they knew someone was going to get killed. They warned the county several times, but no one seemed to care until two young lives were ended due to their negligence. It was amazing how fast the county put up warning signs and how the road was quickly repaired and paved once Dawn Marie and her friend where killed. Warnings were given, but pure negligence prevailed!

One more phone call came early Saturday morning, the day after the accident. The phone rang. My husband said that it was my brother. My brother I thought, I had not heard from him in many years. His sweet words run through me like a fountain of peace and comfort. I remember he kept calling me sweetheart over and over. I had never heard him call me that before. It was as though I was hearing the Lord speak to me. I had never heard the voice of the Lord more clearly in my life. He kept apologizing over and over how his family would not be able to attend the funeral and be with us in Colorado at such a tragic time. It was as if he knew the pain and emptiness I was feeling and yet, there was no way he could have. As I hung up the phone I looked up at the wall and fixed my gaze upon a plague.

At Christmas time, my parents had given me a plague with Jeremiah 29:11 inscribed on it. The plaque was nice, but I did not put much meaning to it at that time. I read the scripture, thought it was a good one, hung it on the wall and never gave it another thought. However, God new the magnitude of this verse for my future. The scripture ***Jeremiah 29:11 states, "For I know the plans I have for you," declared the Lord, "plans to prosper you and not to harm you, plans to give you hope and a future."*** This verse – now hidden in my heart – needed something to teach me to continue to love the Lord, not to blame Him or be angry with Him. Scripture was not what I wanted at that time of my loss, but as time went by, it was my strong tower. It helped me when I was down, and when Satan attacked my thoughts and prayers. This verse carried me during my darkest periods of sorrow. The Lord did not take my precious daughter away from me to hurt me! The Lord did not *cause* this accident to happen! The Lord's plan was not to harm me; even though, I felt my life had been destroyed.

Father, why this verse today? I was hoping this was all a nightmare! Father, I sit on the edge of my bed feeling sick, numb, and torn to shreds and try to reading your blessed Word. Father give me strength today because I have none!

The Lord is omniscient. He puts people and things in our lives at just the right time. The plaque was originally supposed to hang in my office at work, but instead, it landed on the wall right beside my bed. How convenient on this given morning to look up, after hearing the words of comfort and support from my brother, and read Jeremiah 29:11. How abundant are God's blessings.

Friends, I will never forget these two phone calls; first, from my nephew and then, from my brother. Although I received many other calls too, these two were special and embedded in my memory. Did you receive phone calls that stood out amongst the rest? Perhaps, it was a special visitor rather than a call. Either way you must hold on to precious words that can lift you up. I challenge you, today, to find a life scripture. Pray and ask the Lord to reveal a verse or two in his Holy Word that you can study and apply daily as you struggle to heal through your deep, dark tunnel of grief.

Thank you Father for your words of wisdom. It is only because I have hope in you that I can endure such pain and agony. Open my heart, ears and mind to know your compassion truth and love. Help me to understand why I am experiencing such a loss and great pain. Father, why? Why, now! Why me!

The Dark Tunnel of Grief

Cousin Daniel sitting bottom middle

Anna Veal

Journal   Date: _____

The Dark Tunnel of Grief

Planning the Funeral

It is Saturday and less than twenty-four hours since my daughter's departure from this world into the serenity of peace of eternal life with her Lord and Savoir. I know that I should be celebrating her life now, but how? How do I put my own selfish feelings aside and celebrate my loved one's life? Today will be filled with people, more phone calls and planning. I cannot think straight! I need to contact the other families involved with the accident: The driver in the on-coming vehicle and the parents who lost their daughter, the passenger, in Dawn Marie's car that night. What will I say to them? Will they yell at me? Are they angry with Dawn? Where will I begin?

Lord, please wake me! I have had enough! My eyes are not really open are they? Pinch me, wake me from this nightmare, please Lord, I beg you!

I am in shock, they say; I feel out of control and cannot think straight. I have never had to plan a funeral. Where do I begin? What do I do? Our family was so blessed to have had people available who knew how to plan, what to gather, and what questions to ask. God really put some very special people in our lives at this tragic time. My husband was my note taker. Without him and his note pad, I would not have known where to go or what to do. I was pregnant, remember, so he kept reminding me to eat and drink water; he wanted both of us to stay nourished. Planning the funeral was like watching a horror film starring our family. I felt like I was on the outside watching as we all sat around the table discussing what verse would be printed on the program. What would be said in the newspaper? What color and style of casket would be selected? A group of us went together to choose a casket. We agreed on a maroon casket that had pink accents. Dawn was not a girly-girl so I am not sure if pink is what she would want, but that is what we chose, and it was beautiful. Her preference might have been a casket shaped like a racecar or maybe, a black and white one accented with musical notes. Maybe she would prefer a different color or style. How do we know when the person is not alive to ask? What outfit should I select for Dawn Marie to wear? Do you bring undergarments and hose? I don't know; I have never had to do this before. Maybe, none of it matters. They asked me to provide lipstick

– what color? Dawn never wore a lot of makeup. I did not want her all made up. Do we buy her a new outfit or put something she already had on? Does she need shoes? I know this all sounds so crazy, but I was so unsure. I put some things in a bag and somehow they got to the funeral home. Dawn was beautifully dressed; her face and hair were perfect. The feeling of seeing her was overwhelming and too hard to digest. My little girl died on a Friday night around 7:35 and we did not lay eyes on her until late Monday after she was already prepared and in the casket -- I about fell over at first sight. Seeing her lay peacefully made it all become real. This was really happening; there was no turning back. This was not a dream, but a real life nightmare!

Father, why do we have to be the ones to go through such a tragedy? Why our family, Father? Haven't we been through enough! I thought once Dawn Marie graduated from high school and had her eighteenth birthday she was safe from harm! We had a deal, Father! Didn't we?

You see, Dawn Marie's uncle died at seventeen, just thirteen years prior to Dawn's death. I was also pregnant at this time with my second child Adam. It was as if time cruelly took us back and replayed the nightmare of a totally unexpected child's death. Although Dawn's death was not as unusual as her uncle's, it was, nonetheless, just as suddenly devastating. Our family had been through enough already! Why did we have to keep living out this nightmare unable to see our children live a full life that we most certainly expected them to live?

Father, is there a curse on our family? Is there a curse on our young people? Father, I do not know if curses on families are real and alive today like during the Bible times, but if so, I beg of you to please take this curse off our family. Father, we love you and obey you, and we praise you and worship you. Is this enough to remove such a tragic curse? Is it enough? Father, I know I cannot walk away from my faith in you just because I have lost my precious daughter, but I do not know if I have the strength like Dawn Marie's paternal grandparents had through their tragedies. Father, I remember asking how they could have such faith after all they had been through after loosing three of their five children, how can their faith go on Lord, How? They continued to love and trust you; their love for you never slid. Father, I need you to give me that kind of faith and strength. I know I am in denial right now and hoping you are going to allow my darling daughter to bounce through the front door like she always had. "Hi mom, I'm home," was her wonderful greeting. Father, let us hear her words again! Tell me to wake up and show me it is all a nightmare, please!

I had to face the fact that her accident was real. I had to allow myself to start the grief process. I know the Lord was asking me to spend time in His Word, open my Bible and hear what He had to say, but I had no interest in opening up my Bible -- None!

Dawn Marie is safe and sound in heaven now, and I know that for sure. She is protected from the wickedness and evil ways of the world. I could not pray for her to come back. She is exactly where she wants to be. Her earthly life is over, and she will start her eternal life in heaven now. Her time on earth was so short, but her work on earth was done. I had to trust God now!

Father, I cannot concentrate on your Word or any other book for that matter. I feel like I am going crazy. My focus is all on the accident and how awful the loss was. How can I open my Bible and listen, if I am not able to? I struggle reading your Word because I just want my daughter back. I want this all to go away!

The Lord revealed to me that Dawn Marie is in paradise with him now! It is her time of eternal life in heaven, as promised in His Word, to all who believe in Him. ***John 3:16 states, "For God so loved the world that he gave his one and only Son, that whoever believes in him shall not perish but have eternal life."*** Dawn believed; therefore, she will now spend eternal life with her Father in heaven. Our lives on earth are short term, temporary, and a place for us to do Gods work. We are commanded to share the gospel, serve others, and above all, follow His greatest commandment: Love. ***Matthew 22: 37-39 states, "Jesus replied: 'Love the Lord your god with all your heart and with all your soul and with all you mind.' This is the first and greatest commandment. And the second is like it: 'Love your neighbor as yourself.'*** "Once our work on earth is complete, it becomes our time to die in our earthly body and return to heaven with Christ in our spiritual body for eternal life. The Lord was asking me to trust in His Word. This was my season to grieve, and I needed to allow the Word to comfort and guide me through my feelings. We have to remember that God also lost His Son, Jesus. Jesus' death was more tragic, more painful, and far more dramatic than we could ever imagine. No one has ever died a more painful death in history -- no one!

Father, I know you are revealing so much to me, and I want to listen and understand. It is hard to hear your truth when I feel so engulfed with darkness and pain. I want to reach up to you, but I have no energy!

At this point in my grief process, I was so deep in my tunnel of darkness that light was nowhere in sight. Will I ever see the light again?

Dawn age 13 in Wuxi, China

The Dark Tunnel of Grief

Journal   Date: _____

Anna Veal

Lonely Days Ahead

One day seemed like all the rest; the sun rose, the sun set, people came, and people went. The clock obediently ticked minute-by-minute, hour-by-hour; a new day passed just like the last. People went back to work, even I went back after a week or so. I contemplated how people continued on with their lives – playing sports, taking music lessons, shopping -- while my daughter had just died. What was wrong with the world? In my mind, my purposeful life had stopped, so why hadn't theirs?

With an empty heart, my mind became consumed with negative thoughts. My first thought was to run far away. I wanted to escape from the pain and loneness and leave this situation behind. I cried out to Jesus, "Help me escape the pain and loneliness!" My second thought was to turn to alcohol. A strong drink could temporarily kill the pain and agony. But, I contemplated; alcohol would only lead to long-term misery. These negative thoughts consumed me; I needed to be set free! Satan – the father of lies – tried to tempt me with self-defeating ideas that could only kindle the flames of grief. I did not concede to these thoughts; they were only false remedies. Besides, I had a human life growing in me, and I could not harm my unborn baby or myself. **I Peter 5:7 states, "Cast all your anxiety on him because he cares for you."** I thank the good Lord because he was in control, not me. By god's grace, my sanity was preserved. I continued to take my prenatal vitamins and eat a healthy diet. Drinking would have led me deeper into the tunnel; I needed to face this situation with the confidence and boldness of a Christian warrior. Running away never solved a problem; prayer and scripture was the answer. Turning from negative thoughts, I sought the light at the end of the tunnel!

I recited scripture over and over. God was my comfort. He comforted me in times of trouble so that I, in turn, could comfort others in their time of trouble.. I felt the call over and over to open my Bible and read what the Lord had for me! The Lord wanted me to trust him and not to be afraid. God comforted me through his Word! *2 Corinthians 1: 3–4 states, "Praise be to the God and Father of our Lord Jesus Christ, the*

The Dark Tunnel of Grief

Father of compassion and the God of all comfort, who comforts us in all our troubles, so that we can comfort those in any trouble with the comfort we ourselves have received from God."

God is ready to help us in our time of need. Through His Word we receive great understanding and complete comfort. Through prayer, we cast our cares upon Him and rise with renewed strength. Although God makes a way, it is not easy for us to conquer tribulation with human frailty. We need to draw on God's strength to read study or even open the Bible. Life is not easy. We face loneliness, emptiness, and grief, but God is full of compassion for all.

Anna Veal

Journal　　　　　　　　　　　Date: _____

The Dark Tunnel of Grief

Facing Reality with God's Blessings

Today, we must go to Greeley, Colorado and clean out Dawn Marie's dorm room; only eight short weeks ago, we set it up.. I remember that day so well. Dawn, a young lady so full of joy, adventure and a little apprehension exclaimed, "Now Mom, do not expect me to call and talk to you everyday. I will be very busy with my studies and meeting new friends and finding a job!" I just smiled and replied, "Oh, I will understand." However, not one day went by -- not one -- that I did not receive a phone call or an email. She would share with me whatever went on that day: student loan updates, test anxieties, new job opportunities, and all the new friends she was getting to know. It was such an exciting time for both of us. I loved to listen to her share with me each day. I never went to college or lived in a dorm room, so I really had no idea what she was going through or what to expect. Now, these memories are God's daily blessings to me.

A special blessing came the day after we buried Dawn Marie. I woke up super early, and the house was quite. I decided to check on my email as it had been quite sometime since I had even turned on the computer. I opened up my email and right in front of me was a message from Dawn. How could this be? I noticed the date and time. Dawn Marie sent this Oct 26, 2001, around 1:30 pm. She had called me on the same day around 3:30 pm before leaving Greeley to come home. I was sure that whatever was in the email had probably already been shared with me. I opened it up anyway, just to make sure. As I opened the email, these cute smiley faces were dancing around with many different expressions. The music playing in the background was to the theme song of the famous movie "Mission Impossible." As I scrolled down through the smiley faces these words were in large print, "My mission on earth is complete." My heart sank to the bottom of my gut! I had a huge lump in my throat. My heart was beating so fast and loud I began to feel faint. The next words on the email after "My mission in life is complete," were "to make you smile!" I laughed and cried and smiled. My little girls mission was to make us smile, which she did most of the time! But, was this her "mission"? The words were so real. I know

God has a plan and a purpose for each of us, according to Jeremiah 29:11, but I am sure His plan for Dawn Marie was more than just to make us smile. Ironically, this message was sent by my darling daughter just hours before her "mission" on earth, would be complete! God knew this one last email from my daughter would make me cry, laugh and smile. Some people may call this a coincidence, but we, Christian friends, know better; we call this a blessing! Dawn did not know the hour of her death. She most likely sent this because she thought it was cute. However, the Lord knew why she sent it: It would be a blessing engraved on my heart forever. I can still see the email as if it is replaying over and over on my computer screen. This was another special blessing from our Lord and Savior Jesus Christ. Remember to thank God daily for all the blessings you receive.

Other blessings came in due season. Dawn Marie's closest friend's mother had been praying for quite some time for her son's and daughter's salvation, but it was only after Dawn's death that they repented of their sin, accepted Jesus Christ as their Lord and were baptized. I felt so blessed to be a part of their celebration into Christ's family! Her friend's family made a commitment to attend Church and get involved. I know Christ was so pleased with Dawn Marie. While at a baseball banquet with my son Adam, a sweet young lady, who used to play with Dawn while their brothers were playing baseball, approached and shared her story with me. She confided,:"Mrs. Veal, I want you to know this. I used to drive fast and careless, and I never gave it a second thought. Now that Dawn's accident occurred, I have slowed down and become a much better driver!" I gave her a hug and thanked her so much! I never wanted her mom to go through what I had to. It blessed me to know that my daughter's death benefited this beautiful, lively young lady as well. As I watched new life and growth begin in those who had been influenced by Dawn, the pain of losing my Christian daughter diminished as blessings flowed abundantly.

The Lord uses tragedies so we can learn and become better people. The Lord is omniscient. When our faith is tried, according to James 1: 2-4, we must develop perseverance and let Perseverance finish its work so that we may be mature and complete, not lacking anything. I have changed tremendously since my daughter's death. Before, I was a pretty straight shooter. I spoke directly, even if it hurt; I was tough and hard-core. . I was a serious, focused, and goal-oriented person. .One always knew where they stood with me. Now, I have a tender heart with compassion for people. When I hear of a loss, even if I do not know the person or their family, I can cry my eyes out. When speaking to others, I choose words of love and encouragement. I have become a much softer person; I care on a deeper level.

No longer do I see automobile accidents as a big inconvenience caused by people who "should learn how to drive", but as an opportunity for me and my son Anthony, when he is with me, to pray for everyone involved.. We pray for the medical team working on the injured, for other drivers to have patience while the police clear the accident and make their reports, for the insurance companies involved, and most importantly, for the families and the unexpected finances incurred as a result of the accident. I love the new attitude God has blessed me with!

Knowing how to console and support someone, who has experienced a death in their family, can be difficult for the novice. Two years prior to Dawn's death, my neighbor lost her son in an automobile accident. I went to her home right away and helped prepare food for the funeral, but I was a beginner and did not know how to truly support her. However, she knew to lean on Christ and was comforted. When Dawn died, this same neighbor and another knew exactly what to do for us; they consoled with empathy and gave guidance throughout our tragedy. We were so blessed with experienced neighbors!

Now, consider your daily blessings: Did you wake up? Did you arrive safely to school or work? Are you in good health? Do you have food and shelter? Do you have a dollar on you right now? Did you receive a smile or hello from a stranger? Did you receive a hug from your little darlings who love you or pray with someone today? Then you my friend have been blessed! The Bible teaches us about many blessings. ***Deuteronomy 28: 2 states, "All these blessings will come upon you and accompany you if you obey the LORD your God:" Proverbs 28:20 states, "A faithful man will be richly blessed, but one eager to get rich will not go unpunished."*** The Lord wants to bless us in many ways. Will you pray with me?

Father you know how much we are hurting right now. It is hard to even pray. The burden of pain is lying heavy on our hearts. Words cannot describe the loss and sadness we are engulfed with. We cannot see or hear you Lord because the cloud of darkness in our tunnel of grief is surrounding us. Guide us Father to your word so we may experience the many blessings you have provided amongst the pain. Let us see the many positive outcomes that will come from our loss. These blessings will help us to heal and see a better picture than just our tragedy. Let us experience your compassion and love. Forgive us for being blinded by our darkness. Direct the right people in our lives to give us the comfort and support we are in need of. We know you are beside us, guiding us through our grief tunnel, so we can begin to see the light at the end. Amen.

Anna Veal

Dawn-Doherty Drum Line/ Accordion

The Dark Tunnel of Grief

Journal

Date: _____

Anna Veal

Grief a Daily Struggle

Thank you for praying with me. Sometimes when the burden of grief is surrounding us, prayer is the only thing that can lift the darkness so we can begin to heal. Grief is a daily struggle. The hardest thing for me, as a mother, is not knowing what Dawn was doing now that she is in heaven. I know where she is and whom she is with, but what exactly I wondered, is she doing? I do not know why this question haunted me, other than thinking that as a mother, I should know this stuff! For eighteen years I was responsible for her. How can I be her mother and not know what she is doing? This is not natural or fair, I reasoned, to just give up my parental rights in a second! I would daydream about her leading Gods percussion section or taking care of His animals; these were two things she loved doing here on earth. Or, maybe she was enjoying conversation with one of her favorite auto racing drivers, who had died earlier that same year. Just what were her duties?

In one of our Sunday morning adult Bible study classes, a person asked, "What happens when we die?" Another person quoted scripture about we how we are at peace in a deep sleep until our Lord and Savior comes again. Someone else mentioned, we go to paradise with Christ. The Bible has many scriptures to give us direction in our thinking. We need to read it carefully and in context so we do not witness falsely. The Bible can give us the answers we need, and the Holy Spirit will guide us to the scriptures he wants us to read and understand. I found a few versus I want to share with you. In Luke 23: 41b-43, while Jesus was hanging on the cross, one criminal rebuked the other criminal stating, ***"But this man, (meaning Jesus), has done nothing wrong.' Then he said, 'Jesus remember me when you come into your kingdom. 'Jesus answered him, 'I tell you the truth, today you will be with me in paradise.' "*** Daniel 12:2 states, *"Multitudes who sleep in the dust of the earth will awake: some to everlasting life, others to shame and everlasting contempt."* Wow -- deep sleep, paradise, everlasting life, and everlasting contempt we have a lot to still study. You do not have to live in everlasting shame and contempt. The Bible tells us that Jesus loves us, but it also warns of

The Dark Tunnel of Grief

condemnation to those who do not believe in Jesus as the Son of God, who came to take away the sins of the world. Friend, if you do not know Jesus Christ as your Lord and Savior and would like to, please pray this prayer with me:

Lord Jesus, I am unsure and undirected, but with your help I know that I will find the path to your Word and your freedom. Please, forgive me for my sins. I want to have hope and peace in my life. I want to have a personal relationship with you. I want to have understanding of your Word. I give you permission today to enter into my heart. I accept the fact that you were born of the Virgin Mary, died on the cross to save us from our sins, was buried, and on the third day rose again to everlasting life. I want to receive the comfort and your gift of eternal life in heaven. I want to give you my all, Lord Jesus. I want to be born again into a new life with you. I want to die to my old self and rise up to a new life with you: forgiven and free! The only way for me to heal from my grief is to turn it over to you and allow you to work your miracles in my life. Thank you Lord Jesus for accepting me into your kingdom! Amen.

Now that we have taken care of this most important issue in your life we can continue on through our journey together. I want to continue sharing with you some more scripture. I Thessalonians 4:13, which is speaking of the coming of the Lord, states, ***"Brothers,*** *we do not want you to be ignorant about those who fall asleep, or to grieve like the rest of men, who have no hope."* As Christians we have the hope of eternal life with Christ. We know our life here on earth is temporary and that our life in heaven is eternal, with Christ! This passage goes on to state in verse 16 - 18, *"For the Lord himself will come down from heaven, with a loud command, with the voice of the archangel and with the trumpet call of God, and the dead in Christ will rise first. After that, we who are still alive and are left will be caught up together with them in the clouds to meet the Lord in the air. And so we will be with the Lord forever."* My anxiety of not knowing what Dawn Marie was doing was causing me to be stuck in my grief. Verse 18 states, *"Therefore encourage each other with these words."* When we are stuck in our grief and feeling sorry for ourselves, we cannot encourage others. We can hold our child's hand; strap them safely in a car seat, wash their hands continually, and even give them vitamins everyday, but none of these acts of affection and safety compares to the all encompassing love and fulfillment of residing with the Lord forever. My dear friends, so deep in grief, let these words be an encouragement and hope. Can you think of a better place to be than with our Lord and Savior Jesus Christ -- forever? I have allowed the Lord to heal me

I know your heart must be beating a mile a minute, so is mine! You are either really angry at me for quoting so much scripture or you are feeling a tiny bit less anxious depending on where you are in your faith and grief journey. Your loss might have been recent and you are not ready to read these passages. For you, I wrap my arms around you and tenderly remind you that I was not ready either the first time I heard these words. In fact, the first time that I read these verses, it made me feel so confused, but I rested in knowing that those who repent of their sins and believe in Jesus Christ are promised eternal life. (John 3:16, Act 16:31) Dawn repented of her sins, confessed her belief in Jesus Christ, and therefore, has eternal life with her Lord. The security of eternal life with Christ is what Dawn, my daughter did as Christ asked her to do and her mission in life was complete! My conclusion is we do not have all the answers! Paradise, heaven, deep slumber it does not matter they are with the Lord as he promised. I have to be ecstatic for her! It is time for us to release our loved ones and let them be with their Maker. We can begin to heal once we accept the fact that our loved one is far better off now; they have no diseases, pains, worries, anxieties, or other tribulations.

Father, we want to thank you for your blessed gift of salvation and security of an eternal life in heaven. It is still so hard to focus on Dawn Marie's eternal life in heaven when I am so selfishly hurting. I miss her dear Lord! I miss seeing her beautiful smile. I miss her daily stories. She was a young lady so full of life, adventure and love for others. Father I miss her dearly. I need your strength to make it through the day!

The Dark Tunnel of Grief

Dawn Graduation

Anna Veal

Journal Date: _____

The Dark Tunnel of Grief

Trying to Survive

Time passed. Weeks, months and the holidays were upon us. How could I begin to celebrate the holidays? Our family planned to celebrate Christmas at my house this year since my son, Anthony, would be born the week before Christmas. How could I begin to plan, decorate, cook, or even shop for gifts? My heart was still aching! I did not want to hear Christmas carols, or see Santa ho, ho hoing all through the store. How could I avoid all these commercials, flashing one right after the other, reminding us how many days left until Christmas? My son was born December 17, 2001, less than two months after Dawn Marie's death. I experienced both joy and sorrow on that occasion: I received a son, a precious gift from God, but he would never see his beautiful, big sister face to face. How would I tell him about his sister? I was completely numb again. I initially wanted no decorations and no Christmas music playing. I did not want the joy of the holidays in my life this year! As Christmas Day got closer, I realized, however, that Christmas was not about my feelings or me. Not celebrating the joy of Christmas would not be fair to Anthony or Adam, and it would be a terrible disrespect to our heavenly Father who gave the greatest gift of all – His Son. I had to reach beyond my comfort zone and grasp a tiny bit of holiday spirit. I knew that years from now Anthony would ask to see pictures from his first Christmas, just days, after his birth. He would want to have those memories. The family needed happy memories not just gloomy ones.

Father, help me with my sad feelings of loneliness. Help me desire to celebrate the season of your Son's birth. Help me to realize what the holiday season is all about. I ask for forgiveness for feeling so selfish ad pitiful. I do love you and cannot imagine not giving you the celebration you deserve. Give me an opportunity to share your story with someone this season. Help me be a good hostess to my family and celebrate with food and music just like we always have. I love you and Happy Birthday Jesus!

With the help of the Lord, we survived Christmas; it was nice and quiet. Having Anthony in his bassinet near the Christmas tree made Christmas extra special; It was like viewing a live nativity scene. Even though I went through the motions of celebrating Christmas with my family, I felt that Christmas would never be the same again. How could it be without Dawn Marie? We had many traditions that could not go on. One Tradition we had was to listen to Christmas music and make popcorn and hot cocoa as we prepared to decorate the tree. I would first put up the lights and then Dawn and Adam would trim the tree with their favorite ornaments. One Christmas Eve, we put our sleeping bags out under the tree, and we all slept there for the night. Even our dog Butch joined in the fun. These traditions would never happen again.

Father, I know that Christmas is all about you, not us! How can I continue celebrating your special day without my little girl? She loved celebrating Christmas. Father, remember how we used to get in the car and drive around and judge the lighting contest all together. Father, how? Teach me how to go on!

I felt the Lord leading me to dive into the Bible; to really study His Word to focus on scripture for comfort, and to listen with an open heart to Sunday sermons. I just kept hearing over and over the words "Open your Bible."

No, Father, I cannot concentrate; I am having trouble staying focused. I just catch myself daydreaming and my mind drifts off. Is this normal? Father, when will the pain go away? When will I feel like I have my mind back? Will I ever feel normal again? Will I ever have Joy back in my life? When will I see the light at the end of the tunnel, Lord, When?

The Dark Tunnel of Grief

Adam & Anthony December 17, 2001

Journal   Date: _____

The Dark Tunnel of Grief

The First Year

As the days of the calendar progressed and the New Year approached, it continued to bring many challenges. My husband and I had planned to have our formal wedding celebration on March 16, 2002. This date had been scheduled and planned early 2001 prior to loosing Dawn. Dawn was to be my maid of honor and her dress was already bought and hanging in her closet. How could we go on with the plans knowing she would be missing from the line up? My husband had never been married before so we really wanted to have a big wedding for his sake. We decided to go ahead with the plans since so much preparation had already taken place. Next came March 17th. It wasn't just St. Patrick's Day, but Dawn's longtime companion's and best friend's birthday. He was very much a part of our family. Even though we all tried to put on a happy face, we had this huge crater in our hearts. We followed up March with Easter in April. As old as my children were they still looked forward to a stuffed bunny, colored eggs, and candy before going off to church on Easter morning. That year, Easter had one less basket and one less bunny! May was Mother's Day, WOW! I was still a mom and always would be, but the loss I felt that year, and still do on Mother's Day, was painful! Today, I am reminded that I am a mom -- less a daughter. At mother-daughter banquets and teas, I am reminded that my daughter is not her join me. I am blessed, however, to live near my mother, and we continue to attend these functions; I do not think she realizes how painful these events are for me. I am my mom's daughter and she is so proud and happy to have at least one of her three daughters to share mother-daughter events with. I always look around and see the young girls smiling and laughing with their moms. I see the talented daughters performing on stage for their moms and some put on a show together. I breathe in deep, take a deep breath, sip tea do anything I can to avoid those dreaded tears from streaming down my face. I feel the trickle of blood drip as the sharp pain pierces through my heart. Yet, I put on a happy face, and I am glad to attend these events for my mother to enjoy. I do not know how to bail on these special moments when they mean so much to my mom. If just one of my sisters were here, I would find an excuse not to attend. Yet, I know this is a cop out attitude, and will lead me deeper into my dark tunnel of grief. It feels so much easier to run than to face the pain. However, in reality, running from the pain only prolongs dealing with it. My situation is mother-daughter events; yours may be scouting events, couples retreats, or other special events you shared with your loved one. How do we deal with the emptiness inside?

Father, take us by the hand and lead us through our deep feelings of loss as these events come at us each year. Direct our energy in a positive direction. For me, I continue to attend the mother-daughter events, tears or not, in honor of my relationship with my mother. I thank you God that I have a mother who is alive and well to attend the events with.

If you can no longer attend an event due to your circumstances, such as, loosing a spouse or a child, then be creative in how you approach the event. For instance, sponsor a couple that financially could not attend a couple's retreat; share with them how special the couple's retreat was for you and your spouse. Let them know that you want them to have the same opportunity and experience that you had with your spouse. You could borrow a son or daughter, maybe one who lost their mother or father, and take them to an event. Make these memories continue on for those around you. The other suggestion I have is to participate as a volunteer. Help put the event on or participate somehow in the celebration. This allows you to still be a part of the event, but in a different capacity. DO NOT RUN!!! Use these events as an opportunity to reach out to others and spread the gift of joy that the event used to bring to you and your loved one. We can choose to stay in our "pity party," but let me tell you, it is much more rewarding to overcome your fear and pain with joy. Then you can bless others who may be hurting.

Next, of course, we have to deal with the loved ones birthday! What now? Do you just cross their day off the calendar and act like they were never born? Do you view it as one less birthday present to give? Oh come on, how could you!!! This is a real struggle for me as my heart aches year after year as her birthday approaches. For eighteen years we had cake, ice cream, presents and a special meal. August 18th was her special day! What do we do with this day now? Is this just another day? Not for me! I would buy her balloons and flowers and decorate her gravestone. I still plan her favorite meal on that day. This is what made sense and made me happy to always remember her day. On what would have been her twenty-first birthday, I bought extra special balloons; this allowed me to celebrate a milestone that she would have achieved. For me, going to the grave and decorating made me feel close to her. I felt I was still honoring her day.

Although for others, going to the grave is painful and not healthy. Only go if you can go without bringing yourself down. If this is an unhealthy thing for you, do something else. Make their favorite dinner or go out to their favorite restaurant. Do what feels right to you! There is no manual teaching us how to grieve, how to act or what to do with their birthdays or anniversaries; you can celebrate in your own way and make up your own rules! Keep your plans healthy and real! Ask God to help and guide you through your plans for the day. And, please, eat a piece of cake too! What is a birthday without a piece of cake?

Friends, you have heard that time heals, but let me share with you a true statement that I heard while attending a grief workshop: Time does not heal, God does! Believe me friend, God will heal if you reach out and ask to be healed. Each year, I have to continuously ask God to guide me through each holiday, birthday or event when I feel my loss the most. As each year passes by, the joy in my heart deepens as I learn to lean more and more on Christ.

Father, be with us this first year of our loss. Help us know what you would want for us to do to remember our loved ones. Guide us in knowing what is healthy and what is unhealthy. We pray that our families will understand our feelings and how we want to always remember our loved one who has departed this earth. Father, we know you celebrate only a few events such as when we became Christians inviting you into our hearts, and when we come home to be with you in eternity. Help us learn what is significant to you. Give us understanding and peace.

Anna Veal

Journal Date: _____

The Dark Tunnel of Grief

Special People in our Lives

Our family had been so blessed to have many special people in our lives during this tragic loss. Our friends were so dear to us and really provided for our every need. There's one special friend in my life that I had known for about seven years at the time of my loss. We always knew the Lord had put us together for a reason. I met her on her first day back to work after her son's death. I made a sales call, and she was the Human Resource Director who I needed to call on. We spent about two hours together that day. First, we spoke about my company and how it could assist her in her staffing needs. Then she proceeded to tell me about her loss and how she wanted to get involved in the community more. I was involved with a service club, and she wanted to start volunteering in honor of her son. I recruited her into the club, and we became close friends. Seven years later when Dawn passed away she heard the horrible news while attending a club function. She left immediately and came to console me. She knew this would be the hardest thing that I would ever have to experience; she understood the rough road ahead of me. It was on this day that we realized why the Lord put her in my life. He knew that I would need someone who could empathize with me during this tragic time of losing a child. We always had a special friendship, but now, during this time of need, we had an unfortunate common bond. She was a "safe" person to share with. This special Christian lady always had the right words to say to me. We had numerous conversations over tea in her home. We had conversations that led to joy, tears and even laughter. She was quite an inspiration to me. If she could survive such a horrible loss, then I could too! We not only had a common bond in losing a child, we also had a common bond in Christ. As she reached out to me in support and friendship during my time of need, I was given the opportunity to reach out and love another just a few years later: her daughter. My special friend's daughter experienced a deep loss of her own. I was able to share with her in the same way that her mother shared with me. I invited her to a grief support group called Grief Share that God had directed me to.

Grief Share is a program that offers you a place to meet others who are experiencing a loss and processing through their grief. I developed new friendships with so many who were hurting due to a loss. The group is a safe haven for you to share your feelings and pain. Not every loss is the same, but the symptoms are common among all. This group allowed me to be myself, and it kept me from deep depression and medication. The leaders were not counselors or Bible scholars, even though they new the Bible well. These were real people who experienced various losses themselves and who understood the challenges we would be facing. I encourage you to go to www.griefshare.com and find a group meeting near you. This group will help you as you go through the dark tunnel of grief and reach for the light at the end.

Father, thank you so much for the many friendships and people you have put into my life through my tragic loss. Relationships, I know, are special gifts from you and I thank you. I pray now for each and every one of them. Please bless them.

Deuteronomy 31:6 states, "Be strong and courageous. Do not be afraid or terrified because of them, for the LORD your God goes with you; he will never leave you nor forsake you."

Father, I pray for those in need of a friend, one who can listen and understand. Father, lead them to a grief share group or support person who can be there for them. May you guide and direct them to reach out for help. Father, you know my heart and my desires. You know what my first thoughts of alcohol were. Father, help them as you did me to see that drugs and alcohol are negative and will bring them down hard. Father, we want to reach up and be healed, but we are weak. We need you to lift us up. We want your love. Father we are weak, discouraged and mostly afraid to face grief. We need your Word to heal us not false promises from substances that can only cover up the pain not cure it. Help us and direct us, dear Lord. Father, hear our prayers.

The Lord did hear my prayers, and he will hear yours too! Look to the wisdom of His Word. Seek out those friends to help and He will provide for you. **Joshua 1:9 states, "Have I not commanded you? Be strong and courageous. Do not be terrified; do not be discouraged, for the LORD your God will be with you wherever you go."** It is hard to be strong and not afraid because the pain grief causes is so deep it is a like a piercing dagger right through our most precious organ: our heart. We need our friends and family to help us during this painful time in our life. The Lord is with us through Joy or grief.

Father, thank you and please forgive me for not being strong and courageous. Walk beside me as I grieve and am faced with the challenges that go along with grief. Thank you for all your wisdom and guidance. How can I continue to be discouraged when you are with me everywhere I go?

Anna Veal

Journal   Date: _____

The Dark Tunnel of Grief

Milestones

I discovered my mind wandering to the negative more than the positives. No words can explain how I struggled through the darkness grief caused. I became discouraged easily and could not think of the right words to use. I felt so cheated out of life; my little girl was taken at such a young age. I saw so many of her milestones, yet missed so many too; graduating from college, attending medical school, planning a wedding, etc. The medical profession was her dream since she was three years old. Dawn Marie never strayed from her dream. Once in a while, she would say that medical research really interested her, but she never veered from the medical field. Dawn Marie would have been the first to get her doctorate degree in the family I wondered what her wedding or future family would have

The Dark Tunnel of Grief

been line – the grandchildren I would have had. Oh, the pain I felt; it was so intense I could not breathe. Many of you have lost infants or unborn babies; your loss of seeing their milestones was even greater. Those of you who have lost a spouse have missed milestones too: building a home, celebrating an anniversary, retiring, etc.

We all feel cheated in one way or another when we have a loss. We must focus on the good times and memories from the past. I have am thankful for the eighteen, wonderful years that I shared with my daughter, but the pain of feeling cheated by missing out on the milestones in her life haunts me to no end. How do we deal with these feelings? Losing a loved one is such a tragic loss. A dear friend shared a scene of coincidence with me not long after Dawn passed away. My friend was traveling down a busy street in Colorado Springs. She glanced up to the next lane and there was a green Saturn just like my Dawn's car. The words on the license plate read "Dr. Dawn". The young lady inside the car had dark hair pulled back into a ponytail so similar to Dawn's hair. My friend tried to catch up to the car, but with traffic, lost site of it. This puts a smile on our faces when we recall this incident, yet tears of feeling cheated still emerge when we ponder the thought of her dream as Dr. Dawn Marie.

Her passion was orthopedic surgery. She had been through a few breaks in her short lifetime that always required a trip to her orthopedic surgeon for a cast or two. Dawn had a passion to solve medical mysteries. She was a researcher. She was one that would dig deep to find answerers. She was born with a bone deficiency called Asteo-genesis-imperfecto, which caused many of her breaks. She had the kind you outgrow upon reaching puberty, but she never stopped researching the effects of the disease. Dawn Marie had an enlarged rib cage just like her father and grandmother had. We just thought that that was their shape. Through Dawn's investigation and studies, however, she found that this was a characteristic of this bone condition. What a shame to have such a talented, determined young lady taken from us at such a young age. She would have been awesome at whatever she chose to do in life: a doctor of medicine, researcher, or maybe just a wonderful mother. Dawn Marie always said that she would not birth a child, maybe she new something we didn't. Dawn never made it past seven weeks of college, married, or birthed a child, but I know she is in a much better place! The earthly milestones she achieved are minimal compared to the heavenly milestone of eternal life in paradise with her heavenly Father. Wow, now that is a milestone worth celebrating, isn't it!

Father, help me celebrate Dawn's life and not dwell on the feelings of being cheated out of the milestones in her life such as a wedding and childbirths. Father,

I struggle as I watch my friend's children graduating from college, some even doctors. I struggle watching babies being born and yet none call me grandma. How do I get passed these feelings and move into a celebration of Dawn's life. A new child born into your kingdom is something always to celebrate. A joining of two to become three joined in marriage with you as the center is a celebration! Help me to rejoice in these celebrations again. Help me to be the prayer warrior you have asked me to be and pray for each new child and new marriage.

How do we get passed these feelings? We have to remember Gods promise of eternal life and protection. God comforts us in our time of loss and pain. God is always with us, in fact He carries us through the tough times. We have to focus on and be thankful for the many blessings we receive each day.

While focusing on the blessings and not the loss, I was really able to see that in eighteen years my daughter accomplished so much. We actually watched her achieve many milestones in her life. Dawn traveled, both domestically and internationally, and achieved much success in academics and music. Dawn touched so many lives; she helped others discover and develop their talents. What more could parents ask for? We were given a gift from God. The gift was given to us for eighteen years to nurture, cherish and enjoy. This was one of the most precious gifts God gave to us.

Father, forgive me for feeling so selfish. Help me to be thankful for getting to be Dawn's mother. Father, I confess my sins and ask you to continue to do healing in my life. Father, I know that feeling cheated is causing me great pain and anger. How can I move past these feelings and continue on my journey through the dark tunnel to your beautiful light at the end? Father, anger is overtaking me and I feel this strong hold.

The Dark Tunnel of Grief

Dawn & Great Grandma Josie

Anna Veal

Journal   Date: _____

The Dark Tunnel of Grief

Dealing With Anger

Anger is one of the serious stages of grief we go through. Anger can lead us to bitterness, depression and sin. Anger is a feeling that can overtake our body and surround us in darkness. Anger can cut us off from others, at a time when we need them the most. Anger is ugly and causes one to act out of control. All this said, anger is part of the grieving process. Most of us experience some type of anger: anger at God, anger at our families, anger at the situation we are in, or anger over what happen to our loved one. Satan uses anger to get into our lives and take control. **Ephesians 4:26-27 states, "In you anger do not sin: Do not let the sun go down while you are still angry, and do not give the devil a foothold."**

The Dark Tunnel of Grief

During your time of loss, some people do not know what to say or do. Some people may say the wrong things -- you know the ones. You can probably name a few of them. These are some of the ones that I heard: Why are you crying? Your daughter did not belong to you; children belong to God and are a gift. You need to get over it; it has been long enough. She is in a better place now. It's time to stop crying. I know how you are feeling. These are just a few that I experienced. If you experienced a loss, you have a list of your own. Everyone who said these things meant well. They have not walked in your shoes, so they do not understand what they are saying. Your family and friends mean well, believe me! I am almost certain they did not say these things to tear you down. These words, however, can trigger anger in you during your time of grief. We have to pray for those who say things that hurt us. Pray that they will learn to choose their words more wisely next time.

Maybe your loved one died prematurely due to an auto accident, murder, or illness and you have angry feelings toward others involved. Let me share with you why my anger got the best of me. When Dawn's auto accident occurred it was considered gross negligence on the county's part. You see, the county had torn up the road and left the debris. No signs, warning lights, or anything was posted. The neighbors complained to the county, but they did nothing until after the day

Dawn lost control of her car and two young girls lost their lives. This incident was unnecessary and should never have happened. My daughter was not drinking or driving carelessly. If she had seen warning signs, she would have had an opportunity to slow down and take precautionary measures on the road up ahead. This unnecessary road damage made us all very angry. I wanted to post signs stating, "Drive with caution, as the county does not care how safe their roads are." If I posted a sign, would it take my pain away or bring the girls back? No, it would only add negative repercussions to the burden of the loss. I carried this anger for a long time. I showed my anger by yelling and screaming, not at the county, but at those around me. Sometimes when my husband came home or walked in the room, I would let him have it for no apparent reason. He was so good, though. He just walked away and left me alone until I came to my senses. Then, he would try to enter the room again. He really knew when to just leave me alone so that I could work through my anger issues. God made him a wise man, and I am so thankful! My outrages were neither fair to him nor to myself, but I was deep in anger.

Uncontrolled anger can lead to vicious action, which in turn, leads to sin. This is what anger did to me. It did not take much for me to blow up at someone or a situation. I could not control my anger. Anger was taking over me, engulfing me with darkness. Remember, I was a new mother again, so I was dealing with hormones and grief all at the same time. My little Anthony sometimes took the brunt of my anger. I would get upset easily when he cried because I felt like I could not calm him or satisfy his need this feeling of helplessness kindled my unstable emotions. My anger was so out of control that sometimes I would feel my blood pressure rising to new heights. I would rant and rave about how messy the house was, or what was on television, or that a picture on the wall was crooked. The cause was not as important as finding an excuse to be angry.

Prior to Dawn's death I used to read my Bible daily, but now I was unable to make this a daily habit; it would make me angry. I did not feel angry with God, at the time, but looking back, maybe I was. My anger turned on and off like a light switch. One moment I would be raging mad and the next I was fine. I knew doctors could diagnose this problem for this and prescribe a drug, but deep down inside, I knew it was plain and simple: I was angry and trying to process through my grief! How do you get out of the vicious, evil cycle of anger? Pay close attention to your moods. If anger is overtaking you, then please go to the Lord in prayer and ask to have the anger relinquished! Anger is part of your grieving process. If you are angry, do not feel you are alone. All who experience grief can experience a "brief time" of anger. Let "brief" be your key focus during your anger process.

Dear Lord, you know how angry we feel. You know our hearts and our feelings. Father, we do not want anger to rule us! We do not like who we become when we are angry. When we are angry, we sin and say hurtful things to others. Help us dear Lord to recover and move through our season of anger. Help us not to sin. Allow us to forgive others so our anger can be resolved. Although anger is normal, allow us to control it and to understand that it can become unhealthy and sinful if not controlled. Father, keep us balanced through our season of grief. Father, through your power we are starting to see the small light at the end of the tunnel. Help us see your light shining brightly reaching down for us.

As you can see, we need to diligently watch for and guard against anger. Anger is a powerful and destructive force: It swells up inside then slowly comes out and attacks. These attacks are unhealthy and depressing. Sinful anger must be squelched.

Dawn & Adam

Anna Veal

Journal Date: _____

The Dark Tunnel of Grief

Where Is My Brain?

The trauma of losing a loved one is something I had experienced before, but it wasn't the same as when I lost my daughter unexpectedly. This type of trauma can affect each differently. For me, I began to think I was losing my mind. I could no longer focus from the minute I received the bad news. My thoughts were consumed with the accident and the vision of her precious little face in the picture the coroner had shown me. I could not even concentrate on the simple things, such as what to wear, what time of day it was, or what I was supposed to be doing. I was in a comatose stage. I was awake but my brain was missing.

As time passed, I got a little better, of course, but then a memory problem set in. I could not remember to do things unless they were written down on a piece of paper. I carried a note pad and pencil with me for a very long time. If I set an appointment, I would have to write it down on my many calendars. I kept an appointment book in my purse, at home, at work, and in the car. Of course, keep in mind, this was prior to the fancy electronic calendars we have available to us now! I just could not keep things straight unless it was in writing. I forgot so many things. Sometimes, I would head down the road to go to the store around the corner, and I would end up in a different direction heading for who knows where? I was a mess! You could tell my brain was not all there! The bed would be half made, dishes half done, and the dryer door would be open. I would start to make the bed, get distracted, start to do the dishes, get distracted again and then the day kept going on. I am amazed that I got anything done during the first year with so much memory loss and confusion. How I managed to raise my little Anthony that first year is beyond me! I can laugh about it now, but back then it was the most frustrating thing to go through. Had I lost my mind? Well, after a little research and talking with others who had experienced grief, I realized it was all part of the grieving process. It was just another one of those symptoms or stages grieving people go through.

My sister told me about an event that happen during the first year of living without my daughter. She explained how her daughter had watched my newborn while we went to an event with much contemplation. I do not recall the whole conversation, but I remember starring at her with this blank look. She inquired, "What is the matter?" I replied, "I do not remember the event or situation at all." I asked repeatedly and with incredulity, "I let your daughter watch my newborn?" Now, in reality, my niece was capable and old enough, but I did not leave Anthony at all I thought during his first year. I had become a little over protective and was so scared to lose another child that he was with me all the time. After she continued on, I started to vaguely recall the event, certainly not the details!

Today, I try to remember Anthony's first year of development when he started rolling over or sitting up, but honestly and sadly, I have no memory of his first year. I kept his baby book current, however, so I do have a record of his progress and growth. But it is so sad that I was in this trance of grief and do not have these memories. What I do remember is being frustrated with this colicky baby that could only cry and fuss. His colic might have been the result of the anxiety I experienced while carrying him. I was not good at comforting him, but with the Lord's guidance I made it through.

Father, I struggle daily with this memory problem. Lord, am I loosing my mind? What is happening to me? Why am I not functioning like the person I used to be? I am struggling with multi tasking and keeping focused. Father, I cannot lose it now! I have to stay on top of things. I have two boys to raise, and I am still working. I need you to guide me. Father, bring me up to the surface for air! Father, do not let me drown! Father, I do not want to go on medication; I want you to be my healer. I know the doctor can prescribe medication, but Father, I want you to be my ultimate healer! You, Father, I know you have the power, please heal me!

If you are experiencing this frustrating memory loss or confusion, just keep in mind that you are grieving; memory loss and confusion go along with the process. My stage lasted about a year. After that, it was off and on for a while, but I am much better now. Through the power of prayer, the Lord lifted me up without the use of medication. I do not want you to think that I am anti-medication. For some people, it is necessary. For me, I never did well on medication. If there were a side effect, reaction or warning on the prescription, I would experience it. My body just never did well with prescription medications. I stayed clear of all medication, prescribed or over the counter for even the common cold or flu, unless it was an absolute necessary. Then, I had to struggle through the reactions it caused. I really wanted to lean on the Lord for my healing and not on a prescription that I would have to take for who knows how long! The Lord directed me to many scriptures on healing. One portion of scripture that helped me was *James 5:13-16. It states, "Is any one of you in trouble? He should pray. Is anyone happy? Let him sing songs of praise. Is any one of you sick? He should call the elders of the church to pray over him and anoint him with oil in the name of the lord. And the prayer offered in faith will make the sick person well; the Lord will raise him up. If he has sinned, he will be forgiven. Therefore confess your sins to each other and pray for each other so that you may be healed. The prayer of a righteous man is powerful and effective."*

The Lord is our healer! He will lift us up! You see, I was so far down that I could not stand up and reach for the Lord so he reached down and lifted me up! I had to have prayer partners who prayed for me everyday! When I went to church on Sunday, I would hear friends and strangers say to me, "We are praying for you!" I felt those prayers everyday! Prayer is what we need to survive the tragedies that come our way! You see, if we put our faith in the Lord and believe, He is the almighty, powerful God that we can depend on to heal us completely from pain, depression, and even sadness. Do not just pray when you are in need, but confess your sins to the Lord. Pray for others who are hurting and in need of prayer. Prayer, my friend, is the most powerful tool the Lord gave us -- use it! I prayed and others prayed for me. I know now that I was able to survive the loss of my daughter through many wonderful sources: friends, the grief support group, family, and books. My greatest source, however, was and will always be the Lord Jesus Christ in my heart.

The Dark Tunnel of Grief

If you are struggling, I pray that you have a church full of prayer warriors who will take the time to pray with you right now! Ask the elders of your church to pray over you and anoint you with oil so you can receive the healing you need. My friend, if you have faith that the Lord will heal you, he will! If you are on prescription medication for depression, ask the Lord to help you get better so you can quit taking the prescription. Please, pray about it.

Anna Veal

Journal   Date: _____

The Dark Tunnel of Grief

Health and Fitness

Grief and its many stages took a toll on my body. It started to slowly affect my mental capabilities: my thoughts, memory and emotions. What I didn't realize, however, was that it naturally affected my physical health as well. First, I was run down, feeling tired all the time. I know that lack of sleep comes with having a baby, but this was more intense than I had ever felt before. My body was becoming so out of shape, and my motivation to work out was not there. My mood swings were more frequent with greater magnitude in the down direction than the up. I felt so out of balance. My skin was looking dull and blemished. My nails were dry and brittle. The shine in my hair was completely gone!

Father, what is happening to me? I know I am aging but I feel, since the death of my daughter, my body and health have gone down hill completely. Father, I have a new baby. How can I keep up? Oh Father, give me the energy to survive! All that I have gone through is taking a real toll on me. Father, give me the answers please. I have to stay active and healthy for my children's sake. I feel ugly, fat, and plain worn out! What is next for me Lord?

I knew that I had not been taking care of myself like I used to. I needed to get back into taking care of my physical self as well as my spiritual self I knew my eating habits had changed; I ate what was convenient and easy. I was so busy taking care of a new baby and adapting to a schedule of working from home, that planning meals was not a priority. I started praying and asking God for direction. All my life, I struggled with my weight, but now I was feeling not just overweight but pure ugly! **1 Corinthians 6:19-20 states, "Do you not know that your body is a temple of the Holy Spirit, who is in you, whom you have received from God? You are not your own; you were bought at a price. Therefore honor God with your body".**

WOW! I was not honoring God with my body! I was not treating my body like it was a temple! We were bought at a price! If this verse doesn't give you incentive to take care of yourself than I am not sure what verse will. I was convicted! I have to take care of myself but how and where do I begin? **1 Timothy 4:8 states,** *"For physical training is of some value, but godliness has value for all things, holding promise for both the present life and the life to come."* You see, we need to not only take care of our physical body, but our spiritual being as well. I realized that I needed to dig into Gods Word and use it as a guide to make my spiritual self healthy again. Once my soul was aligned with God's Word, I could work on eating better and working out. I needed a little more motivation though. I am a little stubborn! I was talking with my pastor's wife about my issues, and she suggested I visit her doctor. I took her advice, made the appointment, and discussed with the doctor all my symptoms. The doctor did some extensive blood work to weed out any serious health conditions and then made his diagnosis. He found that I was Insulin Resistant. I had higher insulin levels causing a lot of my weight gain and fatigue. I was put on a strict low carbohydrate diet and exercise plan. He used some words that really scared me:" You are a walking time bomb." You see I was not only insulin resistant, but I also had high cholesterol. My bad cholesterol was high and my good cholesterol was at an extreme low. I am the type of person that could have a heart attack at any time. This woke me up, and it woke me up fast! The doctor would give me only two months to get it under control or I would have to take medication to control the insulin levels. Medication? A walking time bomb? I got it!

I agreed to stay on this healthy way of eating for two months. I was what I call a carbo-holic, and now I had to change my habits for a lifetime to stay physically fit. During the two months I exercised every day and stayed on the low-carbohydrate diet plan. In two months I was able to drop over 20 pounds, my hair and nails started to grow at a more rapid pace, my skin became amazingly clearer than ever! I was back in my very small clothes again. More importantly my bad cholesterol dropped, my good cholesterol was back at a healthy level and I was feeling ten years younger! My whole attitude changed, and I started to shake all the anger, depression and other lonely feelings that were weighing me down. I was able to open my Bible again and really get back to normal. Praise be to God once more!

Dear Lord, you are an awesome God!!! You put the right people in my life to direct me back to health. You gave me the ambition and desire to please you and treat my body like it is a Temple! Continue to work in me so I can remain in good health and stay strong to do your work here on earth. Thank you Lord Jesus for your guidance and your love.

Anna Veal

Journal Date: _____

The Dark Tunnel of Grief

Are Christians Pain Free?

I was brought up in a Christian home and went to church every Sunday. My mom was active in teaching Sunday school, choir, playing the piano and organ. Church was a part of my life. I have heard many sermons and attended many conferences and seminars. All that said, I have never heard a sermon preached on "Follow Christ and your life will be pain free: you will be wealthy and live a happy go lucky life!" Get serious! From the moment we accept Jesus into our hearts we become Satan's enemy. We will face more trials and tribulations than we did before becoming a Christian. As Christians we have hope not pain free living. *1 Peter 1: 3 states, "Praise be to the God and Father of our Lord Jesus Christ! In his great mercy he has given us new birth into a living hope through the resurrection of*

Jesus Christ from the dead." 1 Peter 1:6-7, talking about our trials, states, *"In this you greatly rejoice, though now for a little while you may have had to suffer grief in all kinds of trials. These have come so that your faith -- of greater worth than gold, which perishes even though refined by fire -- may be proved genuine and may result in praise, glory and honor when Jesus Christ is revealed."*

When we were living as unbelieving sinners, we were not a threat to Satan because he had us right but now that we are believers in the Lord Jesus Christ and have eternal life in heaven, we become the Enemy's target. Ask any Christian if they are without pain, suffering, struggles or sin! None of us are. If we live without struggles, we will depend on ourselves instead of God. God wants us to be totally dependent on him. We cannot make impossible things happen the way we want using our own resources and strength. *Matthew 19:26 states, "Jesus looked at them and said, 'With man this is impossible, but with God all things are possible.'* "You see, these trials help us stay strong in our faith. I feel so much closer to God now than before I lost my daughter. Keeping your faith, attending church, and volunteering are all wonderful, but the key is your total dependency on God? This starts with a personal relationship with Jesus Christ. A personal relationship is more than just believing in Christ, it's knowing Him as your Lord, Savior, Friend, Healer – your All in All.

Since I was a small child, I believed in the Son of God as my Lord and Savior, but felt my personal relationship deepen to a new level during the time of my loss. You see, it was impossible for me to survive such a tragedy on my own. I needed God to reach down, take hold, and direct me on my path towards His bright light at the end of the tunnel.

Friends, it took me a long time to start to see God's bright light. Now, He shines brightly in my life. I still struggle from time to time; I would be lying, if I told you I didn't. However, I am a much stronger and healthier person, spiritually and physically, today than I ever was in the past. I have learned to depend on the Lord to carry me through life's trials. Become a prayer warrior with me. When the struggles of life hit you in the heart, causing you to loose your breath, kneel down and pray! Let prayer be an over-abundant, habit in your life. Teach your children to pray. When life gets tough, teach them that the tough get down and pray! Learn to pray for others and thank God for your daily blessings. If you are walking through the dark tunnel of grief, I pray that you are now starting to come toward God's bright light and are seen the rewards that await you. You are a child of God's. I will close with my daughter's favorite verse. ***Matthew 5:15-16 states, "Neither do people light a lamp and put it***

The Dark Tunnel of Grief

under a bowl. Instead they put it on its stand, and it gives light to everyone in the house. In the same way, let your light shine before men, that they may see your good deeds and praise your Father in heaven." May you find God's light, keep it, and shine it on others around you who need to see the light at the end of their dark tunnel, too!

God bless you!

Anna Veal

Journal

Date: _____

The Dark Tunnel of Grief

Anna Veal

Journal Date: _____

The Dark Tunnel of Grief

Anna Veal

Journal

Date: _____

The Dark Tunnel of Grief

Anna Veal

Journal Date: _____

The Dark Tunnel of Grief

Acknowledgements

To my Family Mark, Adam, Curtis and Anthony for all their prayers, love, support. They allowed me to grieve and spend many hours working on this book

To the rest of my family who encouraged and prayed for me and helped make this book a reality

C. Renee Yocum- who spent much time editing the first draft and being honest with me

Deborah A. Walsh, my sister, for spending time in prayer as she spent many hours away from her family to edit the final draft

To all my close friends who encouraged me and prayed with me and were there for me when I was at my lowest in life

This Book is Dedicated In Loving Memory of:

Dawn Marie Flory
Kirsten Johanson
Marilyn Flory
Richard A. Flory
Keith J. Flory
Josie Butierries
Ruth Markle
Viola Schlegel
Thelma H. Finsterbusch
Frederick A. Finsterbusch
William Finsterbusch
Larry Young
Dwight Young
Frank Collins

To my nieces & nephews who never made it through birth